Door to Door
With Jesus
In Jesus
Through
The Lord Jesus
The Messiah

Door to Door
With Jesus
In Jesus
Through
The Lord Jesus
The Messiah

Holle Plaehn

authorHOUSE®

AuthorHouse™
1663 Liberty Drive
Bloomington, IN 47403
www.authorhouse.com
Phone: 1-800-839-8640

Published by AuthorHouse   03/22/2012

ISBN: 978-1-4685-5714-5 (sc)
ISBN: 978-1-4685-5713-8 (e)

Library of Congress Control Number: 2012904366

Any people depicted in stock imagery provided by Thinkstock are models, and such images are being used for illustrative purposes only.
Certain stock imagery © Thinkstock.

This book is printed on acid-free paper.

Scriptures used in this book are taken from:

THE NEW OXFORD ANNOTATED BIBLE, third addition, New Revised Standard Version, c. 2001 by Oxford University Press (NRSV)

THE HOLY BIBLE, New International Version, c. 1990 by Zondervon (NIV)

THE BIBLE FOR ALL PEOPLE, Contemporary English Version, c. 2006, American Bible Society, published by G. P. Putnam's Sons (CEV)

You may use up to three chapters of this book for educational purposes. To use larger sections, please contact the author at Holle Plaehn, 2106 South Cushman, Tacoma, WA, 98405.

ACKNOWLEDGEMENTS

I want to thank in a special way the following: Carol Plaehn for editing, typing, ideas, patience, and grace.

Kristin Plaehn for typing, editing, patience, and her ability to put this book into electronic media transmission.

John Maxwell for his help with computers.

Gretchen Plaehn for typing, editing, ideas, and patience.

Andrew Plaehn for his help with contract evaluation.

Nancy Heavey for securing and scanning the front cover.

Carpe Diem Studios in Tacoma, WA for the front cover.

Abi Deleon for providing copies of this book for pre-publishing needs.

The Creative Writing Class at Peace Lutheran Church, Tacoma, WA for their ideas and encouragement.

To Pastor John Stroeh and Pastor-to-be Malcolm Carroll for their spiritual nurture and guidance at Peace Lutheran Church.

Thank you to Peace Community Center and director Bill Hanawalt for touching my life with grace, inspiration, wisdom and with the lives of the precious youth whom they serve.

DOOR TO DOOR
WITH JESUS
IN JESUS
THROUGH THE LORD JESUS—THE MESSIAH

CHAPTER ONE
DEDICATION

I dedicate this book to my wife, Carol Ann Torgerson Plaehn and to our six children—Kristin, Andrew, Gretchen, Janna, Micah and Kerrye. To my Son-in-Law John Maxwell—Grandsons / Granddaughters Nathan, Raiden, Natasha, Jason, Joshua, Owena, Heather, Jaidah, Zaden, Eva, and Jessica.

****

All proceeds after expenses to publish this book are to be given to congregations for evangelism/outreach ministry. You may contact me at the following address to request financial assistance for outreach scholarships.

Pastor Holle Plaehn
Peace Lutheran Church
2106 South Cushman Avenue
Tacoma, WA 98405
(253) 383-1317

DOOR TO DOOR
WITH JESUS
IN JESUS
THROUGH THE LORD JESUS—THE MESSIAH

CHAPTER TWO
THE MOST IMPORTANT CHAPTER—SCRIPTURE
GOD'S WORD MOTIVATES

The following are a few selections from God's Word. I share these because I believe the Scriptures will help to motivate you to reach out with the Gospel of Jesus Christ. These passages are positive/encouraging/motivational in nature. You may read these by yourself or in a group setting. I hope that you will want to read the context of these passages. Take your time. Begin with prayer. End in prayer. God bless and inspire you in your ministry.

(I endeavor to say these words to myself when I awake in the morning. I give thanks to God for another day of grace; then I pray for workers in God's Kingdom beginning with me. I invite you to pray a similar prayer.)

Matthew 9:35-39 Please Memorize
35 Then Jesus went about all the cities and villages, teaching in their synagogues, and proclaiming the good news of the kingdom, and curing every disease and every sickness. 36 When he saw the crowds, he had

2

compassion for them, because they were harassed and helpless, like sheep without a shepherd. ³⁷ Then he said to his disciples, "*The harvest is plentiful, but the laborers are few; ³⁸ therefore ask the Lord of the harvest to send out laborers into his harvest.*" (NRSV)

Matthew 28: 16-20
¹⁶ Now the eleven disciples went to Galilee, to the mountain to which Jesus had directed them. ¹⁷ When they saw him, they worshiped him; but some doubted. ¹⁸ And Jesus came and said to them, "*All authority in heaven and on earth has been given to me. ¹⁹ Go therefore and make disciples of all nations, baptizing them in the name of the Father and of the Son and of the Holy Spirit, ²⁰ and teaching them to obey everything that I have commanded you. And remember, I am with you always, to the end of the age.*" (NRSV)

Mark 1:14-15
¹⁴ Now after John was arrested, Jesus came to Galilee, proclaiming the good news of God, ¹⁵ and saying, "*The time is fulfilled, and the kingdom of God has come near; repent, and believe in the good news.*" (NRSV)

Luke 1:37-38. For context, read Luke 1:26-55.
³⁷For nothing will be impossible with God." ³⁸ Then Mary said, "*Here am I, the servant of the Lord; let it be with me according to your word.*" Then the angel departed from her. (NRSV)

John 4:34-38. For the entire story, read John 4:3-42

34 "My food," said Jesus, "is to do the will of him who sent me and to finish his work. 35 Don't you have a saying, 'It's still four months until harvest'? I tell you, open your eyes and look at the fields! They are ripe for harvest. 36 Even now the one who reaps draws a wage and harvests a crop for eternal life, so that the sower and the reaper may be glad together. 37 Thus the saying 'One sows and another reaps' is true. 38 I sent you to reap what you have not worked for. Others have done the hard work, and you have reaped the benefits of their labor." (NIV)

John 20:21

21Jesus said to them again, "Peace be with you. As the Father has sent me, so I send you." (NRSV)

THE CROSS FOR US AND FOR OUR SALVATION
Matthew 27:45-56

45At noon the sky turned dark and stayed that way until three o'clock. 46Then about that time Jesus shouted, "Eli, Eli, lema sabachthani?" which means, "My God, my God, why have you deserted me?" 47Some of the people standing there heard Jesus and said, "He's calling for Elijah." 48One of them at once ran and grabbed a sponge. He soaked it in wine, then put it on a stick and held it up to Jesus. 49Others said, "Wait! Let's see if Elijah will come and save him." 50Once again Jesus shouted, and then he died. 51At once the curtain in the temple was torn in two from top to bottom. The earth shook, and rocks split apart. ⁵²Graves opened, and many of God's people were raised to life. ⁵³Then after Jesus had risen to life, they came out of their graves and went into the holy city, where they were seen by many people. ⁵⁴The officer and the soldiers guarding Jesus felt the earthquake and saw everything else that happened. They were frightened and said, "*This man really was God's Son!*" ⁵⁵Many women had come with Jesus from Galilee to be of help to him, and they were there, looking on at a distance. ⁵⁶Mary Magdalene, Mary the mother of James and Joseph, and the mother of James and John were some of these women. (CEV)

THE RESURRECTION OF JESUS
Matthew 28:1-10

¹The Sabbath was over, and it was almost daybreak on Sunday when Mary Magdalene and the other Mary went to see the tomb. ²Suddenly a strong earthquake struck, and the Lord's angel came down from heaven. He rolled away the stone and sat on it. ³The angel looked as bright as lightning, and his clothes were white as snow. ⁴The guards shook from fear and fell down, as though they were dead. ⁵The angel said to the women, "*Don't be afraid! I know you are looking for Jesus, who was nailed to a cross. ⁶He isn't here! God has raised him to life, just as Jesus said he would. Come, see the place where his body was lying. ⁷Now hurry! Tell his disciples that he has been raised to life and is on his way to Galilee. Go there, and you will see him. That is what I came to tell*

you." [8]The women were frightened and yet very happy, as they hurried from the tomb and ran to tell his disciples. [9]Suddenly Jesus met them and greeted them. They went near him, held on to his feet, and worshiped him. [10]Then Jesus said, *"Don't be afraid! Tell my followers to go to Galilee. They will see me there."* (CEV)

JESUS' ASCENSION

The promise to us is that we will receive power to be a witness for Jesus.

Acts 1:8. Read Acts 1:1-11.
[8]*"But you will receive power when the Holy Spirit has come upon you; and you will be my witnesses in Jerusalem, in all Judea and Samaria, and to the ends of the earth."* (NIV)

PENTECOST STORY
A powerful story—please read Acts 2:1-47
Acts 2:1-4, 21.
[1] When the day of Pentecost came, they were all together in one place. [2] Suddenly a sound like the blowing of a violent wind came from heaven and filled the whole house where they were sitting. [3] They saw what seemed to be tongues of fire that separated and came to rest on each of them. [4] All of them were filled with the Holy Spirit and began to speak in other tongues as the Spirit enabled them.

²¹ And everyone who calls on the name of the Lord will be saved. (NIV)

Acts 4:31. Please read the context, Acts 4:1-37.
³¹ When they had prayed, the place in which they were gathered together was shaken; and they were all filled with the Holy Spirit and spoke the word of God with boldness. (NRSV)

I Thessalonians 2:2.   For context, please read I Thessalonians 2:1-12.
² · · · ·. we had courage in our God to declare to you the gospel of God in spite of great opposition. (NRSV)

DOOR TO DOOR
WITH JESUS
IN JESUS
THROUGH THE LORD JESUS—THE MESSIAH

CHAPTER THREE
PURPOSE/DEFINITIONS

WHY DID I SELF-PUBLISH THIS BOOK?

My primary reason to self-publish is that I wanted you the reader to reach out with the Gospel of Jesus the Messiah! I want you to follow Jesus into the world—into your parish. I believe that you can be a blessing and that you will be blessed in this adventure with Jesus. I also wanted to stimulate other types of evangelism within you and in your congregation. Be creative. Employ the gifts of the Holy Spirit in outreach.

I realize that many will not go "Door to Door" nor go with the Gospel to family, friends, co-workers or neighbors, but some will. I hope and pray that you are one of those who share the Gospel.

PRAYER

GOD EMPOWER YOU.
GOD GIVE YOU HOPE.
GOD GIVE YOU FAITH IN JESUS OUR LORD.
AMEN.

PARISH

I will use the word "Parish" throughout this book.

Parish in this book means the area surrounding your church building. This area is inside what you consider your boundary—your immediate focus in outreach.

The last congregation I served was Peace Lutheran Church in Tacoma, Washington. The parish for me was South Sprague—to South 15th—to Martin Luther King Way—to South 27th. You might want to draw the boundaries for your congregation—use your common sense.

In a rural area the parish will stretch for miles. Some may describe their parish as the entire town and surrounding area. You make the boundaries—what makes sense to you!

I personally never saw the parish concept as a narrow, limiting boundary. At the last inner city church I served we had many important, helpful members who lived outside our parish. We worked together and God made things happen. I always called on people outside our parish. Nevertheless, I believe the parish concept can be helpful. But there is a danger if we ignore those in our parish. The Gospel is for all. We dare not "step over" those who live near our church. I have watched a number of churches ignore their parish. One day these churches may try to relate to their neighbors and may be too late. Even when you try to relate there are no guarantees. We leave these things to God's grace.

THE GOSPEL

The Gospel is the Good News of Jesus the Christ (the Messiah). God sent Jesus into the world. This Jesus came in the flesh. This one lived on the earth for our salvation. This one lived for us, died for us, and arose for us.

This Gospel is proclaimed and faith in Jesus is the response, the life, and the discipleship for us. God calls us to believe in this loving, caring, present one—Jesus the Messiah.

For me the Gospel is crucial and central. It is that Good News of Jesus I refer to when I use this word Gospel in this book. Christians live in the Resurrection news and in the presence of Jesus.

Christ is risen. He is risen indeed. Therefore, go in peace and serve the Lord. Thanks be to God.

TITLE OF BOOK

DOOR TO DOOR
WITH JESUS
IN JESUS
THROUGH THE LORD JESUS—THE MESSIAH

I selected this title to declare openly the importance of the love of God in Jesus. The powerful witness, the centrality of Jesus for me in evangelism/outreach enables us to go door to door. The power, the promise, and the possibilities are in Jesus. In the Lord's Supper (Holy Communion) Jesus comes to us. As a child I heard the words—"In, with, and under", used to describe Jesus' presence in the bread and the wine. Jesus is mysteriously present. What a wonderful gift of God for us. Yes, the gift is for us and our salvation.

God has sent for all people salvation, hope, joy, and power. We go out in God's power and promise. In Jesus—with Jesus—and through the Lord Jesus—the Messiah.

DOOR TO DOOR
WITH JESUS
IN JESUS
THROUGH THE LORD JESUS—THE MESSIAH

CHAPTER FOUR
DOOR TO DOOR IN YOUR PARISH

Each parish is different. I have served in five parishes—Oil City, Pennsylvania; Houston, Texas; Madison, Wisconsin; Tacoma, Washington and Rock Point, Arizona. Each parish had its unique history, context, people, problems, challenges, and opportunities.

How would you describe your parish? What do you know about your parish? Who lives behind those "doors"? Are you and the members of your church acquainted with people behind those doors? I mean personally acquainted. Yes, the census tract information is helpful. Read it and learn. However, don't stop there. Go out into your parish and learn things from your neighbors you cannot learn in books!

Our parishes are certainly unique—farms, inner city, suburbs, high-rises, business, small communities. Don't leave anyone out.

Example One—In Houston in our church parish there were seven apartment complexes. All had managers who lived in the complex. I visited the managers. Most of them were courteous. Some took my brochures, cards (personal); some allowed me to post a Vacation Bible School poster in the laundry room; one allowed me to put a door hanger on the apartments. One manager needed help with counseling assistance and financial assistance for a resident. If we say that we want to help then we need to be prepared to follow through as best as we are able. I believe this is true in other visits as well. If a family needs food, then do what you can to help them.

Example Two—I visited a few bars in our parish in Tacoma, Washington during the daytime. I got acquainted with the managers/owners. I did not come to drink anything but a soda. In one the lady behind the front counter turned out to be a member of my denomination. At the time, the bar was considered the "murder capital" of the Hilltop of Tacoma which was part of our parish. There was tension in those visits. Community leaders were not pleased with the mayhem that came out of the bar. I doubt if I did much good, but you never know.

Example Three—During most of my time in the thirty-two years that I served at Peace Lutheran Church I visited homes within our parish. I usually went door to door on Tuesday afternoons for about an hour. I walked to the street that I was visiting as this presented opportunities to talk with people on the way or coming home.

One day I saw an elderly man walking slowly down the street—he had a cane. I said hello and then jokingly asked him if he wanted to race. He looked up at me and said that he could hardly make it home. He had just gotten off the city bus—coming home from kidney dialysis. I apologized for my poor humor and we talked/shared. Then I asked if I might pray for him. "Yes please". So near his home—out on the sidewalk—I prayed for him. There are many opportunities to listen and witness and serve.

For me I methodically went block by block somewhat like I would paint a room. When I finished visiting every home in the parish, I would start over again. To complete door to door in my parish took about a year to a year-and-a-half. Sometimes I expanded my outreach pattern to visit homes or blocks that were beyond our parish. Overall, I estimated that in 32 years, I made 23,000 calls door to door.

I hope that this chapter sparks your understanding of how this outreach ministry can be accomplished. The following chapters illustrate the joys and sorrows and the "how-to" of this outreach. My purpose in this book is to be practical in the information that I share.

For many of us the parish has homes—doors! I especially want to encourage you to go door to door in your parish.

DOOR TO DOOR IN YOUR PARISH.

DOOR TO DOOR IN YOUR PARISH!

DOOR TO DOOR
WITH JESUS
IN JESUS
THROUGH THE LORD JESUS—THE MESSIAH

CHAPTER FIVE
IF YOU ASK THEM, THEY WILL COME

If you ask them they will come.

Millard Fuller of Habitat for Humanity said—I have tried asking and I have tried not asking. Asking works better!!!

I suspect Millard meant the words in the context of asking for support and funds to build homes with and for low income people.

I reinterpret the words in another manner. If you ask them, they will come.

Yes, if you ask the neighbor behind the doors they will come—to God's Kingdom, to your parish church—to your door for guidance, for help, for food, for money, and for many other services.

Not all will come but some will; some have, in my experience.

Yes, and I have learned so much from my neighbors. What a blessing of God these neighbors have been for me and for the churches I served.

The goal is to share the Gospel, if possible.

The goal is to touch people with God's concern, if possible.

The goal is to learn from your neighbor, if possible.

This is a "short" chapter in this book, but a very important one. Please read it again. Meditate on the implications for you.

GOD BLESS AND GUIDE YOU.

DOOR TO DOOR
WITH JESUS
IN JESUS
THROUGH THE LORD JESUS—THE MESSIAH

CHAPTER SIX
SURPRISES

Life is full of surprises. Life turns out differently than I expected. Thank God I am not in control. Seventy-five years for me—full of surprises.

No one is at home, but I left a brochure from our church. What a surprise that some time later the family behind that door started worshipping with us. The children came to Sunday School. Later I was introduced to Grandma/ Grandpa. Grandma was very active in our church. I had her funeral. I also baptized Grandpa on his 'death-bed'.

Another family—I knocked on the door—married in another church—one baby very ill—this family had many problems. They became a vital force in our congregation—leaders!

Walking down the street one Sunday afternoon I met a man near our church. I introduced myself. He appeared troubled. I had briefly visited this home in the past and talked with his son. I asked him—"How are things going?" The father shared haltingly that his son had committed suicide one month ago. The father was now cleaning out the home. I am blessed to have talked to this young man and now to talk with the father. At times life is full of pain and sorrow. I pray that both conversations were helpful to them.

I knocked on the door—a lady from Washington D.C. came to the door. She told me that she was new to our neighborhood. Soon she spoke of her loneliness—her fears—she was now in tears. I asked if I could pray for her. So there right outside her door I prayed for her. It was an emotional prayer. I rarely go into a home when I am calling in the parish. I almost never give hugs but I gave her a hug. I invited her to our church—she never came—surprise!

Gang members roamed our parish at will in the late seventies and eighties. They clustered on street corners. I tried to talk with them, especially if I could find one member alone or several in a small group. Not all were friendly but many were—many were! Some asked me to pray for them. Our church built a ramp for a gang member who was shot/paralyzed. After his hospitalization he was responsive to the church for a couple of months—then the gangs drew him back in—a sad surprise. I often saw him in his wheelchair in the neighborhood, sitting in a cluster of gang members. He always acknowledged me with some gesture or words. Two years later he was shot and killed in a gang fight. I attended his funeral and without thinking, I wore the wrong gang color. As I stood before the casket I realized how deadly wrong that could be. Surprise—no one said anything or did anything.

Surprise. I visited a congregate care facility only 200 yards from the front door of our church. What a great ministry emerged for our church through continuous contacts with residents and staff. Our church had worship services there which included special home-made treats. Four to five of the residents often came to our Sunday School and worship services. They enlivened our worship—or not! They asked perceptive questions. They caused a few problems, but not that many. I had weddings and memorial services for them. I also got to meet "The Mother of Jesus" there. Her other name was Evelyn. She often called on the telephone to the church or to my home. I believe my wife had some interesting conversations with her—or not! What a blessing this community of mentally challenged adults, veterans, releasees from our state hospitals, poor and often forgotten people, were to me, to our parish, to our church. Our church was blessed and challenged.

Surprise. I was calling far from our church door. The young man who answered the door on a Saturday morning was well-tattooed—a baby was crying and one was nearby in diapers. He had no shirt on and seemed angry when he came to the door. I told him who I was and I started to say more when he cut me off. "Oh, I know you

Pastor Plaehn. I remember you when I was a kid—my parents brought me to the feeding program at the church and you gave me Christmas presents." Surprise—not what I thought. Another surprise—they never came to our church after that warm visit.

DOOR TO DOOR
WITH JESUS
IN JESUS
THROUGH THE LORD JESUS—THE MESSIAH

CHAPTER SEVEN
DETAILS ON CALLING DOOR TO DOOR

Pray before you begin calling and during your calls. Relax. "This is God's thing not yours".

What should I say when someone opens the door?

Be creative.

There are no golden words that I have ever learned, but here are a few possibilities that I have used over the years.

A. Introduce yourself _____

I am (Pastor) from Peace Lutheran Church—we are located—address. Brief description—"The brown church down the street".

B. I am calling on behalf of our church to:

1. Make contact with our neighbors or

2. To share our church's programs
or

3. To be of service—"May we help you in any way?"
or

4. To ask your help—"How can we be of better service to help our neighbors in this community?" or "To ask your ideas about how to help with the youth of our community?" Then LISTEN. or

5. To get better acquainted with our neighbors.
or

6. To tell our neighbors of—cite a program, special event, Easter services, etc.

C. Remember the Holy Spirit will guide your words

Be clear
Be brief
Be open to what they share
Have a smile on your face
Have a brochure or some newsletter of upcoming events to share

D. Did I (we) remember to pray?!!!

E. LISTEN, observe the new friend you are visiting and their environment. LISTEN.

F. Thank them for their time! Leave graciously, even if they say a negative word/ refuse brochure/are insulting (a very rare occurrence in my experience).

G. As you are walking away, stop and record a few notes on a 4 x 6 card or something small. Name?, exact address?, who spoke with you?, and special information that is helpful for you or the Pastor or someone from the church for a "call back". Use abbreviations that are helpful.

   For example: N.H.—not home
               N.C.H.—no church home
               A star (*) before the address to call on them again

H. After I knock on the door or ring the doorbell, I often back away from the door to allow the neighbor room to speak without being too close. I even walk to the bottom of the steps at times. Give them room! Also, there are people who knock on doors to harm the occupant so be street wise/community wise/culture wise.

I. I rarely enter a home even if asked. This would especially be true for women callers. There are exceptions, for example when I was asked to pray for someone inside or I knew the person. Listen to your inner voice.

J. Return to the church after calling. Go over your notes—fill in the details. Make a copy for your Pastor. Perhaps keep a copy for yourself. Treat your notes as confidential. If a group went out together, take time to come together afterwards and to sit down and share your experiences. Close with prayer. An hour of calling was sufficient for me.

K. If you promise to help someone, please follow through within 24 hours. Did you promise food?—then go buy and deliver it yourself. Return call?—Pastor, please follow up after the groundwork has been laid. The pastor needs to take the time—certainly **call backs** should be made in a week or two.

L. I sometimes sent a letter to those that were identified as call backs. I never did this very much—I believe that a personal contact for call backs is very important. Not all "call back" visits will be positive. Trust God. You are trying!

DOOR TO DOOR
WITH JESUS
IN JESUS
THROUGH THE LORD JESUS—THE MESSIAH

CHAPTER EIGHT
ALLIES / BUDDIES / RESOURCES / COURSES IN EVANGELISM

Are there people who might help you in your calling? I believe that there are.

A. My experience was that I needed to look around. Our national church at one time had a group of college students who would spend three weeks working at a parish. These youth made hundreds of calls with me one summer in Houston, Texas. I was thrilled with their zeal, outreach, and youth ministry.

B. Look to retired pastors and others willing to help. Ask them to help you call in the neighborhood. Explain "the why" to them. I got a positive response from a number of gifted/talented pastors. Thank God. They received no monetary reimbursement. I list a few of them by name

Robert Drewes   John Briehl
Herman Diers   Luther Watness
Eugene Anderson   Elmer Witt

John Reitan
Sigi Sandrock

C. Marion Voxland—I cite her as someone special who came to Peace Lutheran Church as I began my ministry there in 1971. She worked for two months—made a few thousand calls!! What a blessing for our church and for me. She worked as a short time staff person for our national church. I remember that we had an unusual snow storm in January and she persisted in calling every day even in the snow. She was a jewel.

D. Look for part-time or short time staff people. Spend some money on outreach, including staff. Think about free information in the newspaper, purchase ads or set up a web site.

E. Create your own internship program. God's people will serve if challenged and asked. At a neighboring church they created their own internship program. A young lady I know signed up for a year, to learn and to help her church.

F. Teach courses on evangelism in your parish. Not just once a year but a number of times. Look for people within the congregation who will reach out with the gospel of Jesus. Ask them to participate in a class. Teach the class more than once! I did say that didn't I?

G. Hire a part-time staff person to enable the pastor to reach out, to make calls, to be an evangelist. There are dangers in hiring people from the congregation but my experience is that these people are a blessing—not all, but most. Don't hire someone you can not trust. Hire staff after background checks, and contact references. "The wrong person" will cause much grief for the pastor and congregation. Perhaps a contract for one year is a good place to start. Be crystal clear on what you want and expect. Have them share a report each month containing hours served and type of work performed. Before you hire someone, be clear—very clear—in writing what is expected. Have them sign a contract agreeing to strive to meet expectations. Have a committee that includes the pastor to evaluate the person.

Pray for—encourage—the new staff person—they will need the **love** and help of the entire church. Did I mention **love**?!

DOOR TO DOOR
WITH JESUS
IN JESUS
THROUGH THE LORD JESUS—THE MESSIAH

CHAPTER NINE
THE CONGREGATION REACHES OUT

Hopefully the congregation can reach out in "door to door", but you can't wait for a crowd. You start with those God provides. Hopefully, the pastor will lead and set aside the time to go out with those God has provided.

Publicity is needed. Start two months in advance. So often we in staff positions fail to clearly tell the congregation about good programs. Calling "door to door" is a good biblical, Jesus led emphasis. So inform the folks. In the church where I once served there is a small group that goes out on the last Sunday of the month after the second worship service—around 1 p.m. They gather after worship—some bring a sack lunch—a leader clarifies the streets that are being visited. Teams are formed. Some go by themselves. There is 15 minutes of instruction. For example, the instruction covers the purpose of their visits. How? Where? When to return? Prayer.

The group returns at the appointed time and share their experiences. Hopefully one or two will have had visits that inspire. Near the end of this conversation the leader collects the cards of the visitors. A file needs to be kept to keep track of the visits. Make sure the pastor receives information on those homes that should receive a call back. The pastor or some experienced lay person should make a "call back" in two weeks or less on those identified as "call backs".

Results? The results are in God's hands. The congregational members will be blessed. They will learn insights from their neighbors. They will learn that there are neighbors in the parish who will respond positively to the gospel—to an invitation. Some visitors of the church will have had an incredible story to share. Some will have had a negative experience and be hurt. They will need help to understand that a negative experience is not to be taken personally. In some cases help them to remember that suffering by being faithful is a way to help us grow in the faith. "Dear friends, don't be surprised or shocked that you are going through testing that is like walking through fire. Be glad for the chance to suffer as Christ suffered. It will prepare you for even greater happiness when he makes his glorious return. Count it a blessing when you suffer for being a Christian. This shows that God's glorious Spirit is with you". 1 Peter 4:12-14 (CEV)

Going door to door can also be used to share a specific event that the congregation is sponsoring. Vacation Bible School, tutoring, a concert, community meetings, and youth activities are just some programs that you want the parish to know about and to hear a personal invitation. Sometimes you may not even knock on the door but just leave a brochure. This "shot-gun approach" is a first small step in outreach.

As mentioned previously I believe most congregations have excellent programs but we often score an "F" in advertising and letting our neighbors know of these opportunities. Change the atmosphere in your congregation. It can be done with God's help. All things are possible in Christ! "I can do all things through him (Christ) who strengthens me." Philippines 4:13 (NRSV)

I want to close this chapter by lifting up two lay witnesses that I know who went "door to door" in the congregation I served in Tacoma. Byron, in spite of severe "hiccups" that occurred in the last seven years of his life, still went "door to door" for our congregation. What a wonderful example he was to me and to those he contacted. Byron had so many obstacles in his life—a person of color, poor, little education, divorced and often sick. When I had his funeral I told his family and the community of the church—"Byron was a great man." I believe that his family was shocked that I described him in this manner. In God's sight, I believe he was a great man.

A lady named Nancy went "door to door" with her daughter who was in elementary school. Nancy lived in the parish. She worked for the Department of Social Service Rehabilitation Unit. She was so sincere and effective in her calling. She had not been brought up in any church; she often declared that people in the church do not appreciate the grace of God. She died at an early age, in her 40's. The church was packed with people for her funeral service. A number of people testified (many of those with disabilities) about how much Nancy had helped them. When she died, I was in the hospital room with her. I shared the gospel, the grace of God, and Nancy breathed her last breath. Thanks be to God for her and others like her.

DOOR TO DOOR
WITH JESUS
IN JESUS
THROUGH THE LORD JESUS—THE MESSIAH

CHAPTER TEN
CRISIS CALLING

There are crisis moments when "door to door" calling is demanded. <u>You will know when</u> a "crisis" motivates you to go out. I refer to events such as the death of President John Kennedy, 9-11, war, natural disasters in your area—flooding, tornadoes, hurricanes, or earthquakes. Be available—be at the church—open the church for prayer and put out a sign inviting your neighborhood. Call some members on the phone and ask them to help you call as many members, friends of the congregation, and neighbors using the telephone, e-mail, etc. so they know that the church is open for prayer.

When possible, be available: sit on the church steps (entrance)—open the door for a few hours—maybe for the next few days. Be there for those who need help or want to pray.

I also am referring to a local crisis. For example, a young man is shot and killed by a police officer in your parish, a body is found buried in a yard on a street nearby, a house is gutted by fire started by two gang members across

33

the street from your church or any church in the area. These are some crisis incidents that happened to me and I felt compelled to go out on the street to be available. Another bizarre incident in our neighborhood was when there was "a small war" between gang members and a neighborhood U.S Army soldier and his friends from the Army base who came to support him. Over 300 rounds of gunfire were exchanged, yet no one was hit by the bullets! Just amazing! Once again I felt it important to knock on some doors in the neighborhood.

In crisis calling, I suggest that you go door to door with a simple methodology.

- Introduce yourself
- For example, "I am knocking on your door to see how our neighbors are coping since the young man was shot."
- LISTEN
- Some neighbors may not know of the incident. Ask them if they want to know or if they want to talk about this.
- I remember talking at the door for some time with a young lady in high school. She was fearful because a woman had been buried by her husband in a yard on the block near her home. She shared her concerns with me for a long time.
- I remember talking with an older lady. Her husband had helped me many times at the church

with electrical issues. The husband was now deceased. She did not know of the body buried less than 50 yards from her front door. I decided to gently tell her. I believed that older folks do not need to be sheltered from reality. Also I believe that she needed to take safety precautions.

I could tell you many stories but I will stop. You get the idea. I don't recall any neighbor ever being upset with me for knocking on their door in this type of crisis. With some people I talked for awhile—others no—that was OK. I believe that pastors / lay leaders / fellow members / can make ourselves available. The issue in a crisis is—"HOW CAN I (WE) HELP YOU?".

Ask God to help you be servant-minded, compassionate, and wise.

DOOR TO DOOR
WITH JESUS
IN JESUS
THROUGH THE LORD JESUS—THE MESSIAH

CHAPTER ELEVEN
THE BEAUTIFUL GIRL NEXT DOOR

When I arrived in Tacoma with my family in 1971, I began to meet many wonderful people in our parish and beyond. The world is filled with beautiful, precious people—right? Be open to those gifts of God.

In the house next to our church building and parish house lived a beautiful, precious young lady. She was around 20 years old—she lived her life in her single bed. I believe that she had cerebral palsy. She had a contagious smile. She did not speak in words, but she expressed herself with deep sounds that communicated to her guests how she felt.

A younger sister had come to our Sunday School. I knocked on this family's door and that's how I met that beautiful girl next door. I was ushered into the living room where she lived her life. I spoke directly to her and later on she "spoke to me". Always speak directly to "special people" not just to their parents / caregivers. I treasured her winsome smile. I still remember her smile and "words" 40+ years later. I shared Christ with her. I gave her Holy Communion—a tiny piece of bread and orange juice—items she could tolerate with her medications.

At times our youth group visited her. They were blessed. So was I.

There are beautiful girls and handsome boys who are in the same condition. They live scattered in our neighborhoods. Most will not be able to come to our church doors but we can come to theirs. Some doors will open—some will not.

For those homes that are open to God's people there is a ministry to perform—a friendship to be established. The Gospel of God's love in Jesus can be shared. The family may need assistance.

Recently I read a small book by Corrie Ten Boom entitled Common Sense Not Needed. In essence the author urges/invites us also to share the gospel with special needs children and adults. They will listen to the good news, they don't mind repetition of the stories of God's love in Jesus.

One incident out of my own family life was of my nephew Rocky. Rocky is another "special person". Rocky was raised in his own home. My sister has worked hard to provide a life safe and secure for him. I had talked with Rocky many times of faith in Jesus. I mentioned baptism a few times. Many years later I picked up Rocky, accompanied by my parents, from the airport. He walked down the arrival ramp and the first words that greeted me were "I want to be baptized". I was stunned. A few days later after instruction in the Christian faith and telephone calls to his mother and to a church in his hometown that could provide pastoral care—Rocky was baptized—2,500 miles from his home. This was a graceful event for me. Rocky would always say when I asked him about his judgment of an occasion, trip, meal—"marvelous". So it was and still is in my mind.

Not long ago, now as a retired pastor, I was knocking again on the door of the house next door to our church and community center. I thought that I knew who lived there. However, a new family had moved in, and we visited at the door. I spoke of our church's desire to be a good neighbor and helpful to them. Then the lady mentioned another member of the family. "Did I want to meet her?" Of course, and so I was led into a room where a young lady, almost the twin of the young lady I described at the beginning of this chapter was lying in her bed. The time in between the first young lady and the second young lady was 40 years. The day before Easter I stopped by to pray with her and give her a Winnie the Pooh stuffed animal. She gave me a beaming smile. I read her a portion of the resurrection story of Jesus and told her and

her family of the hope in Jesus and a new life in the world
to come. ANOTHER BEAUTIFUL GIRL NEXT DOOR.

MARVELOUS!!

GOD BLESS HER AND HER FAMILY!!

MARVELOUS!!

DOOR TO DOOR
WITH JESUS
IN JESUS
THROUGH THE LORD JESUS—THE MESSIAH

CHAPTER TWELVE
HOW NOT TO VISIT YOUR NEIGHBOR

Recently a salesperson visited my home with "a student". He was friendly, enthusiastic, and articulate. He showed me/told me what he was "selling". I declined—the salesperson persisted—he wondered/questioned why I as a minister, would not support him. (I had thanked him earlier in the conversation and told him I gave my money to my church and to causes I knew of personally.)

He became angry after a number of further attempts to get me to support him with a purchase. He questioned my clear word "no". He left angry, with his body language giving me the signal that "I was a bum"/or worse. His student seemed lost and mystified.

Please. May we represent Jesus well. There are many times people we visit do not want to talk—they are not interested—sick—in a hurry—afraid—suspicious—over-whelmed. REMEMBER YOU ARE A GUEST.

Evaluate your own approach and reaction with others and in prayer.

At another time, I confronted a young man who had eaten at the feeding program at our church. I had no prior conversations with him. I assumed that he had brought alcohol and was now drinking on the church property. The conversation went badly. I believed that my words were not helpful and even appeared Pharisaical. You would think that after 75 years on this earth and receiving so many blessings I would know/do better. Learn from your sins/mistakes.

You and I have been blessed—be a blessing to our neighbors.

DOOR TO DOOR
WITH JESUS
IN JESUS
THROUGH THE LORD JESUS—THE MESSIAH

CHAPTER THIRTEEN
DID YOU MISS ME?

There are all types of outreach (evangelism). Another important outreach ministry is "in-reach". Reach out to those members or friends of the congregation who participated for a while and then they vanished from worship and participation. You had seen them for a while and then they are gone. But are they forgotten? Does anyone care? How about you—pastor—member of the community?

The "vanished" are also precious in God's sight. These too are ones for whom Christ died. I realize some people do not notice when people vanish or are no longer participating. However I believe a few of us do notice. What do we assume?

I have heard some "experts" say that after three Sundays of non-participation by those who were active before—a call by a pastor or some concerned member is needed.

Here is an example of a conversation that you might initiate.

A. "(Their Name) this is (Your Name) from (Church Name). I wanted to call and see how you are doing. I haven't seen you recently and I wanted to know if you are okay."

B. Then, Listen!

C. Their response will often be a surprise to you.

D. You will hear from the "vanished" that there are serious issues that are behind their lack of participation. Not all responses indicate a serious issue—Praise God—but for a significant number a problem is occurring.

These problems may vary from "being hurt by some members"—to marital or family problems—to sickness—to a misunderstanding—to economic issues and on and on.

There are many life issues that stifle and disrupt our faith and draw us away from God and His church. Encouragement is then important. You recall that Jesus visited the disciples who were behind locked doors after his Resurrection.

This visit/telephone call/contact helps reveal our concern—yes, God's concern—for them. This is also a difficult life and who among us has not deeply appreciated a contact. One of the older ladies in our church, a dear, sweet saint often sent letters to our church family. The letters were sincere, thoughtful, and often long hand written epistles. I received a few myself. Why not find out your own, God-given way to reach out to people.

I have tried often to visit people in our parish that I had not seen for a while. Many of these calls were unannounced.

In my own life I remember a Good Friday morning when I was behind a "closed door" i.e. my office door in the house our church used for offices/gathering space. I was depressed/low in spirit. I heard something—yes, there it was again—a faint knock on the front door. I made my way down the dark hall—I opened the door—I looked straight ahead—no one. Then I looked down. Behold—an angel of compassion. A small neighborhood child, reaching her hand out to me, she gave me a gift—flowers—precious flowers she picked herself—a bouquet of dandelions. I took her gift. I was uplifted. God cares—even for me!

I know we are concerned that the "vanished" will be embarrassed or angry. However, let that be. I am hoping that the Holy Spirit will help the "vanished" sense your concern/compassion. As a Pastor I may have more leverage but a layperson has more "clout" with the "vanished". Take the leap of faith and reach out. Some will be absent for other reasons—just let that be. You did reach out.

For a number of years our leadership team at the church, after prayer, began a time of "concerns" of the parish. A major part of this agenda was to ask if we as a community needed to be concerned for members or friends of the parish who had not worshiped for a number of Sundays. At times I shared a few names. I asked if someone could contact that person or family. I tried to never let this agenda item be long or delve into gossip. The council secretary took no notes. I asked that this entire conversation be confidential among us. Yes, there are dangers here, but the greater danger is that we/I pretend that all is well and never reach out to hurting members and friends of our church.

In conclusion, once a person is absent from worship/participation for three months or more, they probably will never return. Three weeks' absence is a flag I suggest you not ignore. Lost sheep—estranged sheep—bruised —overwhelmed by the world—need a good shepherd to seek them out—a good shepherd like you!

You may want to read Luke 15. Here are a few verses from that chapter.

"Tax collectors and sinners were all crowding around to listen to Jesus.
So the Pharisees and the teachers of the Law of Moses started grumbling, 'This man is friendly with sinners. He even eats with them.'

Then Jesus told them this story:
If any of you has a hundred sheep, and one of them gets lost, what will you do? Won't you leave the 99 in the field and go look for the lost sheep until you find it? And when you find it, you will be so glad that you will put it on your shoulder and carry it home. Then you will call in your friends and neighbors and say, 'Let's celebrate! I've found my lost sheep.'

Jesus said, 'In the same way there is more happiness in heaven because of one sinner who turns to God than over 99 good people who don't need to.'

Jesus told the people another story: What will a woman do if she has ten silver coins and loses one of them? Won't she light a lamp, sweep the floor, and look carefully until she finds it? Then she will call in her friends and neighbors and say 'Let's celebrate! I've found the coin I lost.'

Jesus said, 'In the same way God's angels are happy when even one person turns to him.' "Luke 15: 1-10 (CEV)

DOOR TO DOOR
WITH JESUS
IN JESUS
THROUGH THE LORD JESUS—THE MESSIAH

CHAPTER FOURTEEN
SISTERS AND BROTHERS

If you "knock on doors" you will soon visit with brothers and sisters from other churches—other Christians.

My approach is to inform them that I am so glad that they belong to _____ church. I urge them to support their church with their talents/gifts/attendance. I knew most pastors/ministers in my last parish. I often mention my knowledge of their pastor and church. In most cases I can praise their pastors and speak well of them. I thank them for their discipleship. Somewhere in the conversation I make it clear that I (we) do not proselytize but we recognize all Christians as brothers and sisters in Christ. I view them as friends in Christ.

After calling on the same streets for 32 years, I know these fellow Christians in a personal way. I became close to a few of them. No one ever joined our church from this group. I never encouraged this. However, I was glad to speak well of their church and/or pastor and urge them to be faithful. As you reach out in your parish, what will be your approach? Be ready to encourage. I believe that you can be helpful in promoting more cordial, ecumenical relations on the grassroots level.

DOOR TO DOOR
WITH JESUS
IN JESUS
THROUGH THE LORD JESUS—THE MESSIAH

CHAPTER FIFTEEN
MAYBE THEY ARE NOT YOUR BEST FRIENDS

A word of warning, or is it advice? I rarely call on people with a Rottweiler or a German Shepherd in the yard or a clearly marked "Beware of Dog" sign. Many people have watchdogs these days. I tell people who might call on the people with dogs "God will reach them another way". I walk on to the next house. True, I have called on and even challenged dogs but I am less mobile in my old age and the dogs are more ferocious. Use common sense.

Recently my wife visited a new neighbor with a baby gift for the soon to be mother. My wife opened the gate of their fenced yard. A German Shepherd immediately bounded out of the house. Within seconds, my wife was bitten in the hip. The aftermath was a visit to a nearby clinic, a tetanus shot, cleaning the wound, and two hours of time at the clinic. The neighbors came over later and apologized. The expectant mother cried and we became worried for her. I have never been bitten by a dog in forty plus years of calling on people, but it can happen. Please be careful.

I have been guided or have at times ignored the sign—"No Soliciting". I don't feel I am soliciting. I am not "selling" anything, only sharing God's good news. However let your own conscience be your guide.

DOOR TO DOOR
WITH JESUS
IN JESUS
THROUGH THE LORD JESUS—THE MESSIAH

CHAPTER SIXTEEN
FAMILY, FRIENDS, NEIGHBORS AND
CO-WORKERS

I have spent much time in this book urging you and me to go "door to door" in your parish. Now I urge and encourage you and me to reach out to our families, our friends, our neighbors and our co-workers; yes even "strangers".

In my and my wife's immediate and extended families there are many who are not active in a church. Their standing before God is another matter—God alone judges the hearts and lives of people. I don't doubt that many outside the organized church are believers in Jesus—God.

However our role as a disciple is to "go with the gospel". I can reach out to family—even my own. This has not been easy. I am a shy and fearful person. I don't want to offend my family. My family knows how "poor" I am in living out faith in Jesus. Nevertheless, I can talk, share, and urge them to hear the Gospel. I am glad that I had conversations and sharings with my father. He was such a quiet man, but when I was in college "we talked". On the back porch of our home one hot Texas day 50 years ago, I asked him about his beliefs. My father told me for the first time that he prayed for me daily. That day he shared his trust in God with me. I came away inspired and relieved. He witnessed to me in his own way and I was blessed.

I remember a conversation 40 years ago that I had with one of my wife's sisters and her husband. I agonized beforehand, but finally I went alone to their home and we talked around their kitchen table. We talked about faith in God, Jesus and the church. I was so fearful beforehand. Nevertheless, I was glad I shared with them. I don't recall any observable results (changes). Later on, I was asked to have one of their funerals.

Recently my brother died. According to medical science, we both were diagnosed with an incurable cancer called multiple myeloma. We are all dying, but some of us have heard the words of our impending death from the oncologist more than once. We know. My wonderful, loving, caring brother would often say "anyway" before getting to a point. "Anyway" I am so glad in our "last" years we shared about God's love in Jesus. I was inspired to hear my brother "Busty" (N.L. Plaehn) say before going into a coma—"I believe" in God and Jesus. I shared this final conversation at his funeral service. In his own way, he was witnessing to his family, friends, neighbors and co-workers who crowded into the mausoleum.

So I pray—urge—you and me to follow Jesus, pray for opportunities. Take advantage of the time God gives you to witness, to care and to share. Leave the results to God.

The opportunities are there. God help us to care enough for people that we will proclaim the "abundant life" Jesus provides. Jesus said—"I came that they may have life, and have it abundantly". John 10:10. (NRSV)

Consider one final example. Twenty-five years ago I flew back to Madison, Wisconsin to give testimony for a friend I met in the county jail. I was the part time chaplain at the Dane County Jail in Madison. The head officer, a Christian man, gave me permission each week to visit men in their cell block. I was allowed to go into the cell block; then the door was locked behind me and I visited with each prisoner as long as they wanted to talk. I was so thankful for this correction officer. A prisoner named Odell had been charged with murder. Odell sought me out; we talked often. He asked for Baptism. The wonderful, dedicated head officer in the jail granted me permission to baptize Odell. So now years later Odell's parole hearing was occurring. I was there as a witness.

Before I left my home in Tacoma, Washington I prayed for the opportunity to share Christ. At that time I rarely traveled by air and almost never talked with anyone. On the way to Madison the man next to me on the airplane seemed to want to talk; so I mostly listened. He was concerned about his sexuality. We talked for a long time. I endeavored to tell him of the God who is above all these perplexing questions bothering him. The Good Shepherd Jesus would direct and guide him.

I was weary when I got to Madison—sharing—witnessing —caring is exhausting at times. After the hearing for Odell I was on my way home. Eventually he was paroled. As I sat in the Madison airport a young woman in her 20's was seated a few feet away and she was crying. What could I do? I found the courage to walk a few feet, and sit next to her. I asked her if I could help. I told her I was a pastor. She began to share her hard life as a dancer in a bar—rejection—pain—betrayal—poverty. Now she believed that she must return home to Tennessee. She was fearful about how she would be received.

Our flight turned out to be the same commuter plane to Chicago O'Hare. I was astonished that I was seated one row behind her in the plane. I asked if she wanted to talk more; she did. We got a seat exchange from a fellow passenger. For 45 minutes we talked and we prayed. I told her of Jesus the Messiah who would help her. We prayed some more. I gave her a hug at the airport. I never saw her again—I don't know her name. But I am glad that we had our time of sharing. I had asked God to give me an opportunity to witness and to share and God did hear my prayer.

"Ask, and it will be given you; search, and you will find; knock, and the door will be opened for you. For everyone who asks receives, and everyone who searches finds, and for everyone who knocks the door will be opened." Matthew 7:7-8. (NRSV)

DOOR TO DOOR
WITH JESUS
IN JESUS
THROUGH THE LORD JESUS—THE MESSIAH

CHAPTER SEVENTEEN
DON'T BE AFRAID

Throughout the Bible believers in God are exhorted—"Don't Be Afraid." Have faith in God. Trust God. Stand fast. Move on out. Press on.

A case in point is the story of Joshua. Again and again Joshua hears from God, Moses, and the people not to be afraid. To me there must have been evidence of fear in Joshua to receive the same message on numerous occasions. Joshua was a leader, long time follower of God, a companion of Moses on Mt. Sinai when God revealed Himself in powerful ways. Nevertheless, even after years of service and unique opportunities of grace from God, Joshua is reminded/urged/supported with the message—"Don't Be Afraid." "The Lord gave this command to Joshua son of Nun: Be strong and courageous, for you will bring the Israelites into the land I promised them on oath, and I myself will be with you." Deuteronomy 31:23 (NIV) Also consult Joshua 1.

In the New Testament from Mary the mother of Jesus, to the Twelve Disciples, to the rank and file believers the message was the same—"Don't Be Afraid." So I say to you "Don't Be Afraid". Reach out. Step out. Share the Gospel. Tell people of God's love. Yes, even go "door to door".

Will "fear" arise within you? I suspect fear will arise. I can't remember a time when I went door to door that a tinge of fear, or more, did not come. However God's love conquers our fears and we go—we reach out—we step out. When I was in the 6th grade I was sure that I had tuberculosis. A friend and I had been selected to have another TB x-ray after the first one revealed a problem. In those days if you had tuberculosis you often had to leave home and live in a hospital in San Antonio or maybe even Arizona. My fears were unfounded. The second x-ray indicated there was no problem for my friend or myself. When I was in Seminary, my first visit for a pastoral counseling course was to a large hospital in Columbus, Ohio. The person selected for me was a TB patient! As I walked down the hospital ward hall my fears ignited. I walked past the room. I was only able to take a glance at the patient and then I walked on and on. Finally, I turned around and walked back to his door and the good Lord helped me to walk into his room. We had a good visit.

I have read that there are over three hundred and sixty five times in the Bible that followers of God are exhorted—"Be Not Afraid". So I remind you and me—"Be Not Afraid."

Move out with faith in God. Jesus is with you. You can, in Christ, care and share. Go to the One Who in love "casts out" our fears.

DOOR TO DOOR
WITH JESUS
IN JESUS
THROUGH THE LORD JESUS—THE MESSIAH

CHAPTER EIGHTEEN
HOW TO USE THIS BOOK

There are a variety of ways to read and use this book.

1. Personal reading and personal application is the most obvious. Read. Meditate. Act as the Holy Spirit directs and empowers you. Open your eyes to new possibilities that the Holy Spirit will reveal to you.

2. A group from your church can study/reflect/ share. Together the group can decide their course of action, I suggest that the group pray together and reflect on chapter 2: "God's Word Motivates". Not every chapter is worthy of an entire session—for example chapter 15, "Maybe Not Your Best Friend". Most of the chapters are brief. Probably six to eight weeks (meeting once a week) would be sufficient for a study group. At least one or more of these sessions can be devoted to our experiences during the previous week when we shared the gospel.

3. Pastors can conduct a course for the congregation using this book, the Bible, and their own supplemental materials, experiences and approaches in evangelism. A course in evangelism should be taught more than once a year.

4. Have your church leadership team read this book together. Spend 30 minutes at the beginning of the leadership meeting in discussion. Have evangelism be a central theme for the year.

5. Evangelism/Outreach is a priority item. The church as a missionary organization can be stressed every year. Use your prayerful creativity in the Holy Spirit to lead you in your parish. Be expectant. Be faithful. Believe.

DOOR TO DOOR
WITH JESUS
IN JESUS
THROUGH THE LORD JESUS—THE MESSIAH

CHAPTER NINETEEN
OPEN LETTER TO CHURCH LEADERS

Bishops, Leaders of the Church, Deans, Church Presidents, and other Shepherds . . . .

God bless you and uphold you. Being a leader according to the Bible is an important position in God's church. Serve in and through the Spirit of God. This chapter is an "open letter" that I hope you will read and implement in your jurisdiction. Only by the grace of God will this book and the vision it presents ever get in your hands to read and to be acted upon.

The vision is for you to lead your churches in a series of <u>symbolic acts.</u> I am thinking of the symbolic acts of the prophets or Jesus for that matter. Symbolic acts are powerful if God's Spirit is in them. If God is not in the actions then we are left with Pharisaism of the worst sort.

The vision I suggest for prayerful consideration is for you to lead in outreach/ evangelism, visiting every synod/ conference/jurisdiction under your oversight. Lead us out of the church building into our neighborhoods. Visit the neighbors with love, concern, the Gospel, a brochure on the church, and an offer to assist the neighbor if needed;

I strongly suggest that <u>you not teach us</u> but <u>lead</u> us into the neighborhood. I believe that most of our church members have been instructed—we need to move out with faith in Jesus.

Your role would be to dedicate six days a month for this vision. Each day you would go to a church and lead that church community visiting "door to door" in that parish. Having led God's people for one day, you would then go on the next day to another church. Once again, each month you would give leadership to a "door to door" outreach ministry for six days. Guide us, lead us until you have visited all the churches in your oversight.

For those leaders with a large number of churches you might need to take a year or two for this Vision of Symbolic Acts. For even larger jurisdictions you may need to limit your presence to a couple of churches in each jurisdiction. However, ask all the churches in this jurisdiction to participate, being led by their own leadership.

CONGREGATIONAL AGENDA

The agenda for such a visit could be as follows:

9:00a.m.	Members/Callers Arrive—receive information on route and materials/partnering if desired/ simple suggestions on what to do.
9:30a.m.	Prayer Time
9:45a.m.	Leave for Outreach/Calls/Door to Door.
11:00a.m.	Return/Prayer/Sharing of experiences.
12:00p.m.	Lunch for all who are visitors or anyone who wants to participate
1:00p.m.	Second Group of Members/Callers assembles (perhaps new people). Receive assignments/information/ etc. Prayer for the Holy Spirit's guidance.
1:30p.m.	Leave for Outreach/Calls/Door to Door.
2:45p.m.	Return/Prayer/Share experiences.
3:15p.m.	Members/Callers are free to return home.
6:30p.m.	Third Group of Members/Callers assemble. These calls in the evening would be to recent guests in worship, families who have shown interest in the church or people in need of visitation, both members and non-members. Take along brochures, prayer books, etc.
6:45p.m.	Prayer, Leave for Outreach/Calls/Door to Door. Make two calls. Some of these types of calls could be preceded by a telephone conversation.

| 8:30p.m. | Return/Prayer/Sharing of experiences. |
| 9:00p.m. | Return Home. |

This vision in some ways is simple. Indeed so were the Biblical, symbolic acts. The need in our parish—in our church community—is great.

Jesus said "The harvest is plentiful but the laborers are few; therefore ask the Lord of the harvest to send out laborers into his harvest." Matthew 9:37-38
NRSV

Prayer is essential—so is action.

GOD BLESS YOU.
LEAD YOUR FLOCK.

DOOR TO DOOR
IN JESUS
WITH JESUS
THROUGH THE LORD JESUS—THE MESSIAH

CHAPTER TWENTY
AHE'HEE' THANK YOU

I close this sharing with thanksgiving. Thanks be to God for the grace, love and mercy I have received day after day—year after year. I have been blessed and refined by God's love in Jesus the Messiah.

I thank my wife Carol who has been a partner with me in the Gospel. I thank my children—Kristin (John), Andrew, Gretchen, Janna, Micah, and Kerrye. They are the treasure—the wealth of my life.

I thank my parents Ed (Pop) and Clara (Holle) Plaehn who sacrificed so much for me. They gave me the education and the enriching opportunities they never enjoyed. I honor my "elder" brother N.L. Plaehn (Louise) and my sister Beatrice Hudson. Each year their relationship and friendship have enriched me more and more.

I thank Carol's parents Ed and Meta Torgerson for welcoming me into their family—and for their large, varied, extended family who accepted me, loved me, and encouraged me.

I have had the privilege of being a part of many congregations on my journey:

A. St. Paul's Lutheran Church, Brenham, Texas (Home and first congregation)
B. Good Shepherd Lutheran Church, Columbus, Ohio (Seminary home church)
C. Good Hope Lutheran Church, Oil City, Pennsylvania (Internship congregation)
D. Park Place Lutheran Church, Houston, Texas (First Call in the ministry)
E. St. Mark's Lutheran Church, Outreach Pastor/ County Jail Chaplain, Madison, Wisconsin
F. Peace Lutheran Church, Tacoma, Washington (32 years).
G. Salishan Lutheran Mission, Tacoma, Washington (volunteer pastor)
H. Community Christian Church, Federal Way, Washington (volunteer pastor)
I. Soldezin Ba Hooghan at Tse Nitsaa Deez Ahi (House of Prayer), Rock Point, Arizona (volunteer pastor)

Each congregation helped me to grow in service and in witness for Christ.

In Rock Point, Arizona I was privileged to serve with and under Dine' (Navajo) leadership. They taught me so much through their friendship. I endeavored to learn the Dine' language—I failed, except to learn a few words. The Dine' still accepted my poor attempts to communicate. I once read that the Dine' do not use the words "Thank You" as frequently as some people in U.S. society. A linguist of the Dine' language stated that the Dine' assume that you understand that they are thankful when you perform a task for them or give them a gift. However if the Dine' are bubbling up with thanksgiving—if they want to say thank you from the depths of their hearts—they will say—Ahe'hee.

Ahe'hee'—Thank you! So I say to God and I say to all who share the Gospel of Jesus the Christ, Ahe'hee'.

Ahe'hee'—from the bottom of the heart.

God Bless You.

Go in peace and serve and witness for the Lord.

"May God be gracious to us and bless us and make his face shine upon us, that your ways may be known on earth, your salvation among all nations. May the peoples praise you, O God; may all the peoples praise you." Psalm 67: 1-3 (NIV)

ABOUT THE AUTHOR

Holle and Carol Plaehn served in God's ministry for 40 years. Holle was born and reared in Texas and Carol in Idaho. They met at Texas Lutheran University and were married in 1959.

Holle's passion was to proclaim the Gospel of God's love in Jesus, to evangelize (share the Gospel), and to pay attention to people who are often overlooked in the church's outreach.

By God's grace, Holle and Carol parented six children. Carol was and is a teacher and librarian. They have lived in Tacoma, Washington for 40+ years.

Carol and Holle have been blessed by God.

This book is written to inspire you to share the Gospel.

CPSIA information can be obtained at www.ICGtesting.com
Printed in the USA
LVOW06s2233090814

398251LV00004B/195/P

9 781468 557145